# MAKING SCIENCE WORK

# Light

TERRY JENNINGS

Illustrations by
Peter Smith and
Catherine Ward

RSVP

RAINTREE
STECK-VAUGHN
PUBLISHERS
The Steck-Vaughn Company

Austin, Texas

Published by Raintree Steck-Vaughn Publishers, an imprint of Steck-Vaughn Company

A Mirabel Book

Produced by Cynthia Parzych Publishing, Inc.
648 Broadway, New York, NY 10012

Designed by Arcadia Consultants

Printed and bound in Spain by International Graphic Service

1  2  3  4  5  6  7  8  9  0  pl  99  98  97  96  95

**Library of Congress Cataloging-in-Publication Data**
Jennings, Terry J.
        Light / Terry Jennings : illustrations by Peter Smith and Catherine Ward.
            p.   cm. — (Making science work)
        "A Mirabel book."
        Includes index.
        ISBN 0–8172–3960–X
        ISBN 0–8172–4253–8 (softcover)
        1. Light—Juvenile literature.   2. Optics—Juvenile literature.
    3. Optical instruments—Juvenile literature.   [1. Optics—Experiments.   2. Light—Experiments.
    3. Experiments.]   I. Smith, Peter, 1948–   ill.   II. Ward, Catherine, ill.   III. Title.
    IV. Series:  Jennings, Terry J.  Making science work.
    QC360.J44   1996
    535.2—dc20                                                                                95–11539
                                                                                                      CIP
                                                                                                      AC

## Key to Symbols

"See for Yourself" element

Demonstrates the principles of the subject

Warning! Adult help is required

Activity for the child to try

**PHOTO CREDITS**
Art Directors Photo Library: 20
Belitha Press Limited: 23
B & U International Picture Service: 16 bottom, 25
Celstron: 24 center
© Frank V. DeSisto: 18
© Jonathon Eastland: 8 bottom, 16 top, 20, 28
Image Engineering: 13
Jennings, Dr. Terry: 8 center, 14
Lambe, Dr. Thomas: 24 top
© 1994 Monterey Bay Aquarium: 8 top
NASA: 6 top
Norfolk Seaport Association: 6 bottom

# Contents

# What Is Light?

Light is all around us. We can see things only when light is shining on them. Without light we cannot see.

In the daytime nearly all our light comes from the sun. At night most of our light comes from electric lights. A little light also comes from the stars. In this book we are going to look at how light behaves and some of the things that use light.

**Warning: Never look directly at the sun. It could damage your eyes.**

The setting sun

A full moon

Oil lamp

Reading lamp

Room lamp

Desk lamp

Flashlight

Candle

5

# Light All Around Us

Most of our light comes from the sun or fire. Electricity can also be used to give us light.

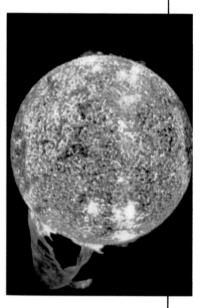
The surface of the sun

Some of the most powerful electric lights on Earth are in lighthouses. Lighthouses warn ships and boats to keep clear of rocks. The lamp of a lighthouse has lenses all around it. These lenses make the light into a bright, narrow beam. The lenses are turned by electric motors. They make the beam sweep around.

People called lighthouse keepers look after lighthouses. They live in the lighthouse. Today many lighthouses do not have lighthouse keepers. They are run by computers.

The lighthouse at Sheffield Island

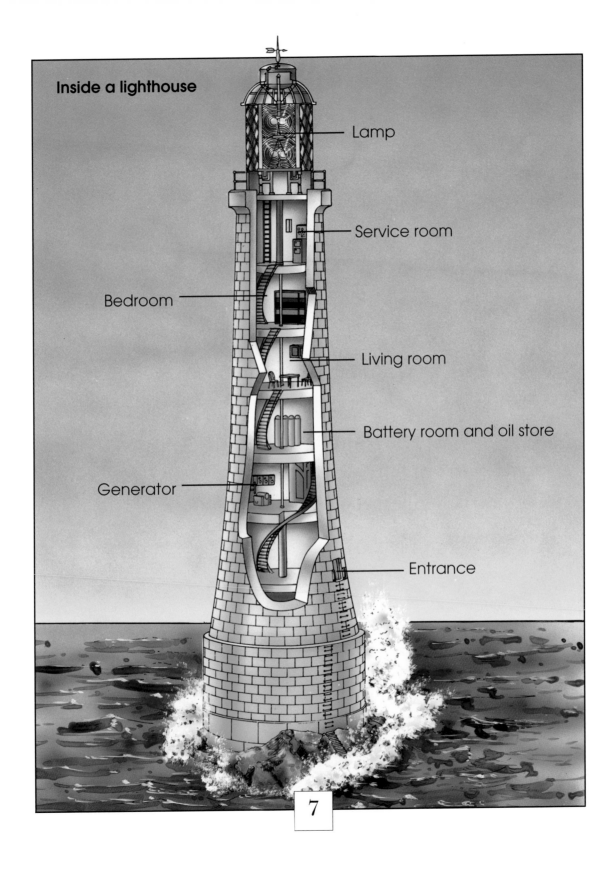

**Inside a lighthouse**

Lamp

Service room

Bedroom

Living room

Battery room and oil store

Generator

Entrance

Sunlight shines through windows. A window is usually made from glass. You can see clearly through most glass windows. Glass is a transparent material. Some materials let some light through. Waxed paper and tissue paper let a little light through. You cannot see clearly through them. Materials like these are translucent. Some materials, like wood, do not let any light through. They are opaque.

An aquarium is transparent.

A translucent lampshade

A ship's mast is opaque.

8

Make a collection of bottles, bags, cans, and jars. Switch on a flashlight. Lay it on a table so that it shines toward you. Hold each container up to the light. Which is transparent, translucent, or opaque? Make a chart of your results.

Light travels in straight lines. It cannot go around corners. Sometimes in a sunny room you can see specks of dust floating in the air. They are lit up by light moving across the room. You can see the straight path of light.

You can see for yourself how light travels. Find three square pieces of thin cardboard, all the same size. Draw lines across each to find the center. Make a pencil hole in the center of each piece.

Center

Pencil

Hole

1 Draw lines to find the center.

2 Make a hole. with a pencil.

Ask an adult to push a knitting needle through the holes to make sure all three pieces of cardboard are in a straight line. Use modeling clay to keep them upright. Stand a piece of black paper behind the last card. Shine a flashlight through the holes. Where does the light fall? Move the middle card a little to one side. Shine the flashlight through the holes. Where does the light fall now?

3 Ask an adult to push needle through holes

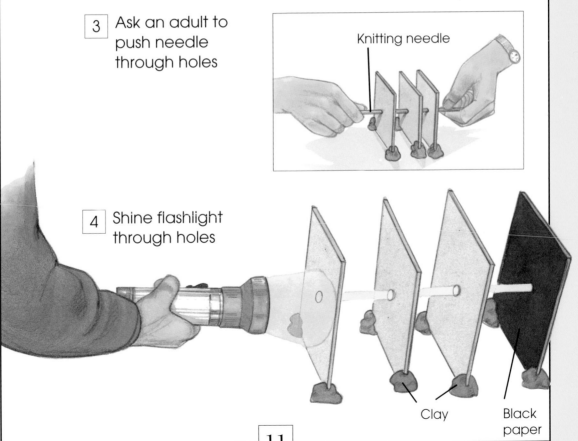

Knitting needle

4 Shine flashlight through holes

Clay

Black paper

# Lasers

A laser sends out a very narrow beam of light. This beam is very powerful. Some laser beams can cut a hole in a thick steel sheet. Some lasers have a crystal, such as a ruby, in them. Others have special dyes or gases. Electricity or light is put into the laser. The crystal, dye, or gas makes light come out of the laser in a narrow beam. Factories use lasers to cut metal, glass, or cloth. Doctors use low-powered lasers to carry out delicate operations. Lasers are used in compact disc players and at supermarket checkouts.

Using a laser to cut metal

Mirror

**Inside a gas laser**

Lasers create the colored lighting at some concerts and stage shows. Laser beams can also be sent along thin glass fibers. They carry radio, television, and telephone messages.

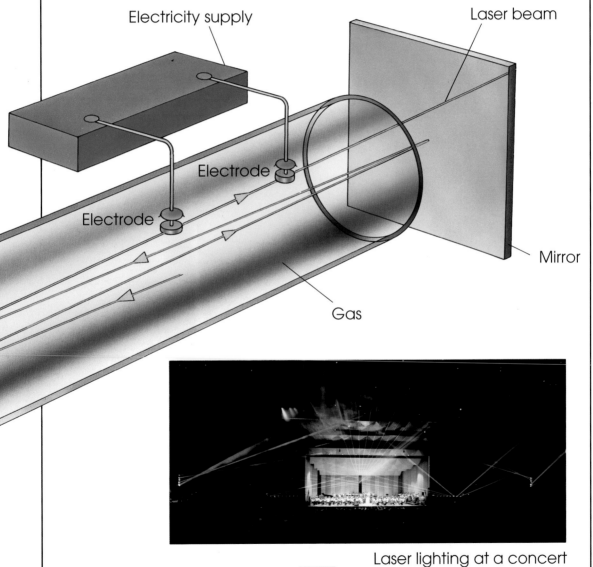

Electricity supply

Laser beam

Electrode

Electrode

Mirror

Gas

Laser lighting at a concert

Light can bounce off surfaces, just as a ball bounces off a wall. This is called reflection. If a surface is rough, like a brick, light bounces off in all directions. If a surface is smooth and shiny, it can be used as a mirror. In a mirror we can see the images or reflections of things held in front of it.

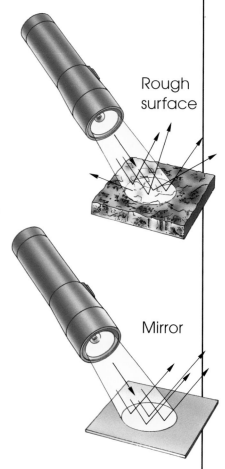

Rough surface

Mirror

Mirrors are usually made from smooth glass. Behind this is a thin layer of shiny metal. A mirror can show us what we look like. Cars have mirrors so that drivers can see behind them.

A swan reflected in still water

Collect a group of shiny things. Some of the things you might collect are pots, pans, spoons, cooking foil, and holiday decorations. Look for the shiny surfaces of each. Can you see your face in any of them? Does your face look the same in each object?

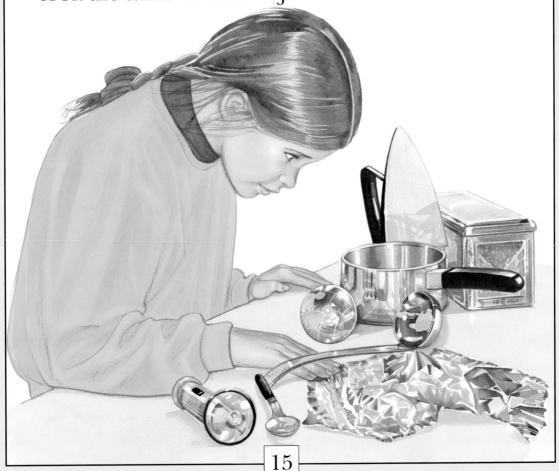

15

# Looking in a Mirror
## See for Yourself

A flat mirror does not show you as you really are. Your image in a mirror is reversed. If you wink your right eye, your reflection winks the left eye. If you touch your left ear, your reflection touches the right ear.

A convex mirror

Not all mirrors are flat. Convex mirrors bulge outward. They make things look smaller but give a wider view. The mirrors in cars and stores are convex mirrors. Concave mirrors curve inward. They make things that are near look bigger. Most shaving mirrors and makeup mirrors are concave.

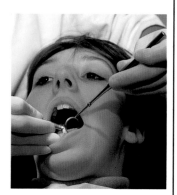

A dentist uses a concave mirror.

Join three flat mirrors with tape. The shiny sides should face each other. Drop tiny pieces of tin foil and colored paper down between them. What do you see? You have made a kaleidoscope.

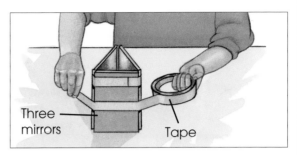

Three mirrors

Tape

1 Join mirrors

A shiny spoon can be a curved mirror. Look at yourself in both sides of a shiny spoon. Are the reflections the same?

Foil

2 Drop foil pieces

3 Look inside

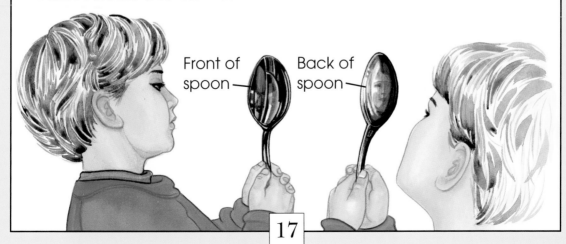

Front of spoon

Back of spoon

17

Sometimes it is useful for us to see over the top of things. A periscope lets you do this.

A periscope consists of a hollow tube. At each end is a mirror. The periscope can be raised or lowered.

A submarine has a periscope. With the periscope, the crew can see what is happening on the water's surface. They can do this even while the submarine is underwater.

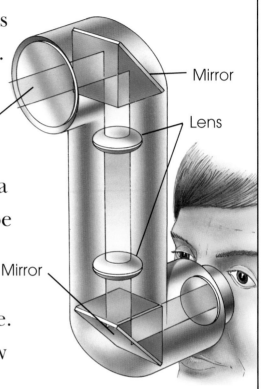

Mirror

Light

Lens

Mirror

**Inside a periscope**

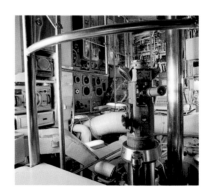

A periscope inside a submarine

Ask an adult to help you make a periscope. You need a cardboard tube. Ask an adult to cut four slots and two round holes in the cardboard tube. Ask an adult to slide mirrors into the slots. The shiny side of the mirrors must face each other. Cover the top and bottom of the tube with black paper. Use a rubber band to hold the paper in place. Look through the hole. What do you see?

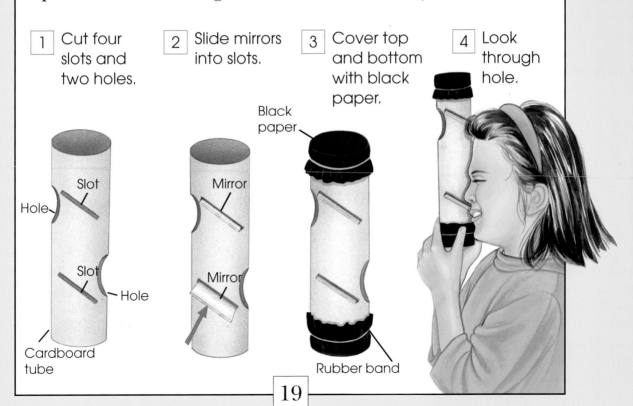

1 Cut four slots and two holes.

2 Slide mirrors into slots.

3 Cover top and bottom with black paper.

4 Look through hole.

Slot

Hole

Slot

Hole

Cardboard tube

Mirror

Mirror

Black paper

Rubber band

Everything that is in the light is bright. A shadow is a dark area. It is formed when something blocks the light. The shape of a shadow is roughly the shape of the object or person that made it. You can see this for yourself by making shadow puppets.

In bright sunshine dark shadows are formed.

1 Cut shapes.

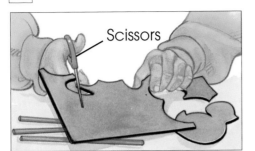

Scissors

2 Tape sticks onto shapes.

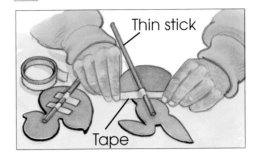

Thin stick

Tape

Cut out some shapes from thin cardboard. Tape sticks onto the shapes to make shadow puppets. Shine the light of a desk lamp onto a wall. Hold the shadow puppets between the lamp and the wall. Look at the shadows they form. Cut out some shapes from colored cardboard or plastic. What color shadows do they make?

3 Hold shapes between lamp and wall

Desk lamp

Shadow puppet

# Refraction and Lenses

Light does not always travel at the same speed. Light moves faster through air than through water. When light changes speed, it usually also changes direction slightly. This makes things seem to bend. You can see this if you look at a drinking straw in a glass of water. This "bending" of light is called refraction. Lenses work because of refraction. This is because light travels slower through glass than through air.

Drinking straw

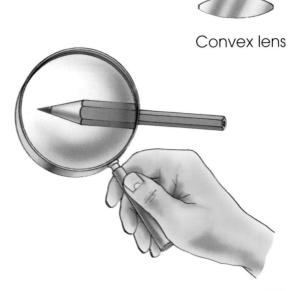

Convex lens

A convex lens is thicker in the middle. It bends light rays together. A convex lens can be used to make things look bigger. It is often called a magnifying glass.

A magnifying glass is a convex lens.

A concave lens is thicker at the edges. It spreads the light rays apart. If you look through a concave lens, things seem smaller.

Concave lens

We have a convex lens in each eye. These lenses help us to see. Many other objects have lenses in them. Eyeglasses, telescopes, binoculars, and cameras have lenses in them.

Eyeglasses have lenses.

Using binoculars

**How the eye works**

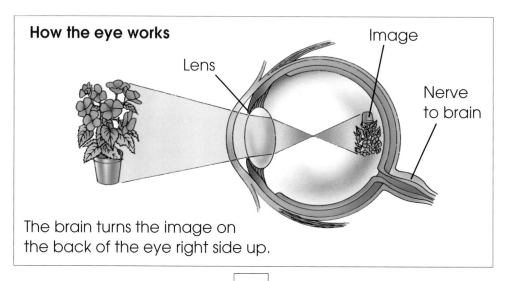

Lens

Image

Nerve to brain

The brain turns the image on the back of the eye right side up.

**How a telescope works**

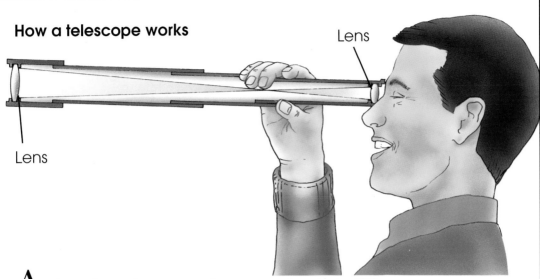

Lens

Lens

A simple telescope has two lenses. They make things seem closer. A large lens at the front bends the light rays together. They make an image. A small lens makes the image larger. Binoculars work like two small telescopes, one for each eye.

A microscope also uses lenses to bend light. Some microscopes have many lenses. A microscope using light can make things seem up to 2,000 times bigger.

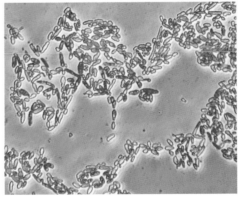

A microscope makes things like these cells look bigger.

F ind a clear glass jar with a screw-on lid. Fill the jar with water. Hold it over a newspaper. The type looks bigger. The jar of water is acting as a convex lens or magnifying glass.

Jar of water

Lid

Drop of water

You can use a drop of water as a simple lens. Find a clear plastic lid. Make a small hole in it with a thumbtack. Cover the hole with one drop of water. Look through the water drop at a magazine. See how your lens makes the type seem bigger.

26

Make a simple telescope. Take two magnifying glasses. Hold one in each hand. Look through the two lenses together. Can you make things look bigger or smaller? Change the distance between the magnifying glasses. What differences do you see?

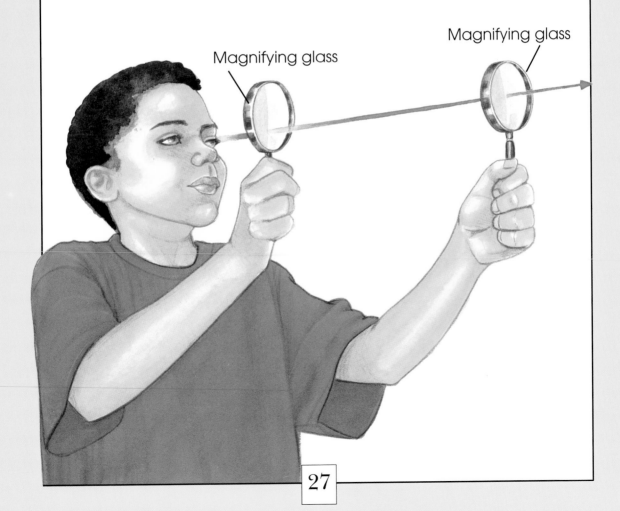

Magnifying glass

Magnifying glass

Cameras are used to take pictures called photographs. On the front of a camera is a convex lens. It makes a picture appear on the film inside the camera. When you look into the viewfinder, you see the picture the camera will take. When you press the button to take the photograph, the shutter opens like a little door. The shutter opens for only a fraction of a second. It lets a little light onto the film. There are chemicals on the film. These are changed by the light.

Taking a photo

The film stores the picture that the camera took. The film has to be developed to see the pictures on it. When film is developed, it is put into special chemicals. These chemicals make the pictures show up. Then photographs are printed from the film.

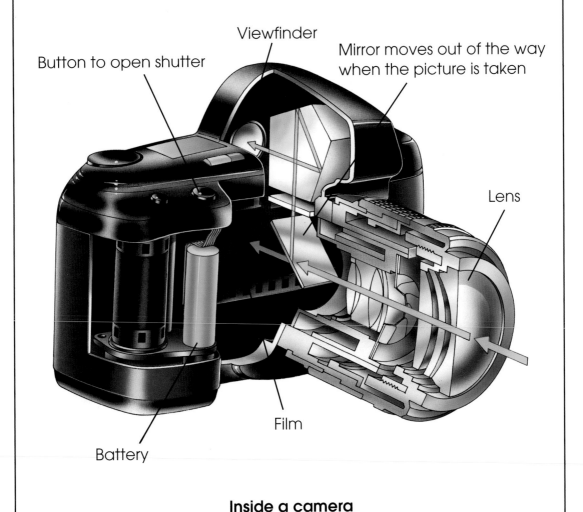

Viewfinder

Button to open shutter

Mirror moves out of the way when the picture is taken

Lens

Film

Battery

**Inside a camera**

## Make a Pinhole Camera
## See for Yourself

The first camera did not have a lens. It was a box with a tiny hole in the side. Light passed through the hole. It made an upside-down image inside the box.

Make your own pinhole camera. Cut one end of a shoebox. Paint the inside of the box black. Let the paint dry. Tape in a window of tracing paper. In the middle of the other end of the box, use a pin to make a tiny hole. Put the lid on the box. Hold the camera up to your eyes. Point the pinhole at a table lamp. What can you see on the tracing paper?

Shoebox

Tracing paper

Tape

Pinhole

# Glossary

**Binoculars** An instrument with lenses for both eyes that makes distant objects look nearer.

**Camera** A device for taking photographs.

**Electricity** A form of energy that can be changed to light, heat, sound, or movement energy.

**Energy** What is needed to change things or make things move. Light, sound, heat, and electricity are forms of energy.

**Kaleidoscope** A tube containing mirrors. You see colorful patterns when you look in it.

**Laser** A device that sends out a narrow beam of powerful light.

**Lens** A curved piece of glass or clear plastic. Some lenses make things look bigger.

**Light** A form of energy you can see. The sun and stars give off light.

**Lighthouse** A tower with a bright, flashing light to guide and warn ships.

**Magnifying glass** A lens that makes objects look bigger.

**Microscope** An instrument that makes tiny things look larger.

**Mirror** A smooth glass or metal surface that reflects things.

**Opaque** Describes a material that does not let light through.

**Reflected** What happens to light when it hits something and then bounces off.

**Refraction** The way in which rays of light change direction slightly when they pass from one substance to another.

**Shadow** A dark shape formed when an object blocks light.

**Telescope** An instrument with a lens for one eye that makes distant objects look clearer.

**Translucent** Describes a material that lets light through but not enough to see through it.

**Transparent** Describes a material or object that lets light through so that it is clear enough to see through.

# Index